The Life of a Saint
Ignatius of Loyola

Text and Illustrations by Miguel Berzosa Martínez
Historical commentary by Antonio Pérez Gómez
Translated from the Spanish by Brian Edwards

ATF PRESS

Adelaide
2009

ISBN: 9781921511644

Cover design by Maggie Power, Jesuit Communications, Australia

ATF Press
An imprint of the Australasian Theological Forum Ltd
P O Box 504
Hindmarsh
SA 5007
ABN 90 116 359 963
www.atfpress.com

This pictorial life of Ignatius of Loyola was originally produced by Ediciones Mensajero in 2002, in Bilbao, Spain. The Australian Jesuits, in collaboration with ATF Press, have adapted the publication for an English-speaking audience. Brian Edwards translated the Spanish text of Miguel Berzosa Martínez and Angel Antonio Pérez Gómez. Jesuit Communications Australia assisted with the cover design.

Saint Ignatius' story continues to provide inspiration to people seeking to discover the path that God has chosen for them. We hope this booklet will help school students and others appreciate Ignatius' journey, and understand more about the foundation and mission of the Society of Jesus.

Original title *Ignacio de Loyola* by Miguel Berzosa Martínez.
ISBN: 84-271-1668-3
© 2002 Ediciones Mensajero, SAU, Bilbao.
Email: mensajero@mensajero.com
Web:http://www.mensajero.com

YOU'VE GONE TOO FAR THIS TIME, IÑIGO. WE START WITH A FESTIVAL QUARREL AND END UP RUNNING FROM THE POLICE LIKE CRIMINALS.

STOP COMPLAINING. JUST KEEP A COOL HEAD AND WE WON'T GET HUNTED DOWN LIKE LITTLE BIRDS.

YOU WON'T BE ABLE TO GET OUT OF THIS SO EASILY. BY NOW EVERYBODY IN AZPEITIA WILL BE TALKING ABOUT YOUR LITTLE STUNT. WHERE WILL YOU GO? TO AREVALO?

NO. TO PAMPLONA.

PAMPLONA? AND DO YOU THINK IT'LL BE BIG ENOUGH TO HIDE IN?

HIDE? NO, I'LL GET PROTECTION AT THE BISHOP'S PALACE.

GOOD HEAVENS! AT THIS RATE NOTHING'S GOING TO STOP HIM.

IT WAS FESTIVAL 1515. IÑIGO DE LOYOLA SOUGHT CHURCH PROTECTION FROM THE POLICE. INTERVENTION BY THE EPISCOPAL VICAR ENSURED THAT HIS YOUTHFUL ESCAPADE DID NOT LAND HIM IN PRISON. SOME MONTHS LATER IÑIGO RETURNED TO AREVALO UNDER THE PROTECTION OF DON JUAN DE VELAZQUEZ, CHIEF TREASURER TO KING FERDINAND.

FOLLOWING VELAZQUEZ'S DEATH, IÑIGO WAS WELCOMED AS A GENTLEMAN INTO THE HOME OF THE DUKE OF NÁJERA.

ROBBERIES AND STREET FIGHTS WERE FREQUENT. IÑIGO ONLY GOT INVOLVED IN AN INCIDENT IF HE WANTED TO.

HELP! STOP THIEF!

I MUSTN'T RISK MY LIFE IN STREET FIGHTS. I HAVE TO THINK OF MY FUTURE AND MAKING A FORTUNE. MY PLACE IS AT COURT.

AT VALLADOLID, TIME WAS TAKEN UP WITH PARTIES, GAMES AND TOURNAMENTS. IÑIGO, WITH NO HOME OF HIS OWN, WAS CONFIDENT HIS GALLANTRY WOULD LEAD TO A GOOD MARRIAGE.

EVEN HERE, HIS EXCESSIVE AMBITION WAS HIS UNDOING.

SAY, MARTIN, ISN'T THAT LADY PRINCESS CATALINA OF AUSTRIA?

YES, SHE LIVES HERE IN TORDESILLAS WITH HER MOTHER, THE QUEEN, ALMOST LIKE A PRISONER. THEY LET HER OUT TO ATTEND THE GAMES.

ISN'T SHE BEAUTIFUL!

AND TOTALLY BEYOND YOUR REACH.

WITH THE DARING OF YOUTH, AND CONFIDENT IN THE SKILL OF HIS ELOQUENCE, IÑIGO APPROACHED THE PRINCESS. HE TALKED OF TRAVEL AND ADVENTURE, AND DESCRIBED TO HER THE GREEN LANDSCAPE OF HIS CHILDHOOD, SO DIFFERENT TO CASTILE. HE SPOKE OF A FUTURE FULL OF GREAT PLANS AND LOFTY AMBITIONS.

I ADMIRE YOUR GALLANTRY, AND ENVY YOUR FREEDOM ABOVE ALL. MY WORLD IS LIMITED TO THAT LITTLE SPECK OF A PLACE CALLED TORDESILLAS, FROM WHERE I LOOK OUT ON THE CHILDREN PLAYING. SOMETIMES I THROW COINS DOWN TO THEM JUST TO MAKE SURE THEY DON'T RUN AWAY.

AND NOW PLEASE EXCUSE ME. MY BRIEF STAY AT COURT IS OVER. I AM EXPECTED BACK AT TORDESILLAS.

WAKE UP, YOU STUPID BOY. AREN'T YOU LETTING YOUR DREAMS RUN AWAY WITH YOU, CASTING YOUR EYES ON A PRINCESS LIKE THAT?

I'M ALWAYS ASPIRING TO THE HIGHER THINGS, MARTIN, THE HIGHER THINGS.

THE YEARS PASSED. THE DUKE OF NÁJERA CAME INTO CONFLICT WITH PRINCE HENRY, WHO LAY CLAIM TO NAVARRE. A WAR BROKE OUT AND LASTED FAR TOO LONG.

IÑIGO TOOK PART IN THE FIGHTING, MORE OUT OF GRATITUDE TO THE DUKE THAN FROM A FIRM BELIEF IN THE JUSTICE OF THE CAUSE.

THE GARRISON AT PAMPLONA WAS GROWING WEAKER. A LARGE FRENCH ARMY ARRIVED IN SUPPORT OF THE ATTACKERS, AND WITH THEM THOUSANDS OF NAVARRANS LOYAL TO THE PRINCE. IN THE FACE OF SUCH A DIRE THREAT, THE DUKE OF NÁJERA ABANDONED PAMPLONA TO SEEK REINFORCEMENTS, BUT WAS NEVER SEEN AGAIN.

THE SITUATION IS DESPERATE. THE BISHOP AND OTHER OFFICERS HAVE FLED WITH THE DUKE. EVEN THE INHABITANTS ARE HOSTILE TO US. I HOPE MY BROTHER MARTIN ARRIVES SOON WITH SOLDIERS FROM GUIPUZCOA.

LOOK, LOYOLA IS GOING OUT TO MEET HIS BROTHER.

ANOTHER DESERTER.

9

BACK TO YOUR POSTS. THE ATTACK WILL COME AT ANY TIME.

AND THE REINFORCEMENTS?

THERE AREN'T ANY, AND THERE WON'T BE ANY.

ALL IS LOST. THERE'S NO CHOICE BUT TO SURRENDER.

A KNIGHT NEVER SURRENDERS.

THAT NIGHT WHILE ON WATCH, IÑIGO WEIGHED UP THE RISKS: WOULD HE FIGHT TIRELESSLY LIKE A HERO IN DEFENCE OF THE CITADEL RIGHT TILL THE END, OR WOULD IT BE ABSOLUTELY STUPID TO DRIVE HIS MEN AND HIMSELF TO CERTAIN DEATH? DAWN CAME AS HE STILL STRUGGLED WITH HIS DOUBTS.

FIRE AT WILL!

THE BULK OF THE ARMY APPROACHED THE WALLS AND THE ARTILLERY BEGAN TO THUNDER.

HOLD ON, MEN!

THE CANNONS FIRED THEIR DANGEROUS SHOT WITH A DEAFENING ROAR...

LOOK OUT, CAPTAIN!

...SOWING A MESSAGE OF DEATH.

CAPTAIN LOYOLA HAS FALLEN.

HE'S BADLY WOUNDED.

HIS LEGS ARE ALL SMASHED.

THIS IS THE END.

OH, RAISE THE WHITE FLAG!

PAMPLONA HAS SURRENDERED.

COUNT DE FOIX, THE CAPTAIN WHO LED THE FIGHT AGAINST US IS BADLY WOUNDED.

TAKE ME TO HIM. I HAVEN'T ALWAYS STRUCK SUCH A BRAVE ENEMY.

YOU WILL BE TREATED WITH ALL THE HONOURS DUE TO AN HEROIC ENEMY. MY PERSONAL SURGEONS WILL TEND TO YOUR WOUNDS.

I ACKNOWLEDGE YOUR GENEROSITY, BUT WOULD YOU ALLOW ME ONE FAVOUR: LET ME BE TAKEN BACK TO MY HOME AT LOYOLA?

GRANTED.

COUNT, ONE LAST REQUEST.

TAKE THIS.

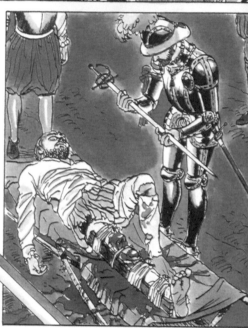

IÑIGO SWUNG BETWEEN LIFE AND DEATH FOR DAYS. HE ENDURED TERRIBLE TREATMENTS WHILE CONSCIOUS AS DOCTORS TRIED TO RESET HIS SHATTERED BONES. AN UGLY BONY LUMP DEVELOPED ON HIS LEG WHICH WOULD PREVENT HIM FROM PUTTING ON HIS BOOTS.

FINALLY, THANKS TO HIS PHYSICAL STRENGTH AND, ABOVE ALL, HIS WILLPOWER, HE BEGAN TO RECOVER HIS HEALTH.

SITTING AT THE WINDOW OF THE TOWER HOUSE AT LOYOLA, LOOKING UP AT THE IZARRAITZ RANGE OF MOUNTAINS, IÑIGO WHILED AWAY THE HOURS, TORN BETWEEN DISAPPOINTMENT AND BOREDOM.

MAGDALENA, AREN'T THERE ANY BOOKS OF ADVENTURE OR CHIVALRY IN THE HOUSE TO LIFT THE SPIRITS OF YOUR BROTHER-IN-LAW?

NONE AT ALL. I'LL BRING YOU WHATEVER I CAN FIND.

THE LIFE OF CHRIST AND THE LIFE OF THE SAINTS. GOODNESS ME! I WOULD HAVE PREFERRED AMADIS DE GAULA, BUT I SUPPOSE ANY BOOKS ARE BETTER THAN NOTHING: AT LEAST THEY'LL BE A DISTRACTION.

IÑIGO READ AND RE-READ THOSE BOOKS, FORCING HIMSELF AT FIRST, BUT LATER WITH GROWING INTEREST, UNTIL AN INSPIRATION BEGAN TO DEVELOP IN HIM THAT TOOK HIM FAR FROM HIS EARLIER THOUGHTS OF HONOUR AND GLORY.

WHAT IS HAPPENING TO ME INSIDE? WHAT GREAT AMBITION IS PUSHING ME TO DO WHAT FRANCIS OF ASSISI AND SAINT DOMINIC DID?

THE DAY'S PASSED AND IÑIGO WAS OBSESSED WITH THESE THOUGHTS. SLOWLY HE FELT PHYSICALLY IMPROVED, BUT THIS WAS NOTHING COMPARED WITH HIS INTERIOR TRANSFORMATION.

MARTIN, I'M WORRIED ABOUT IÑIGO. SO OFTEN I SEE HIM LOST IN THOUGHT, SHUT AWAY IN HIS ROOM FOR HOURS. THERE'S SOMETHING ON HIS MIND.

DON'T WORRY SO MUCH, MAGDALENA. HE HAS JUST SURVIVED A SERIOUS INJURY, AND IT WILL PASS.

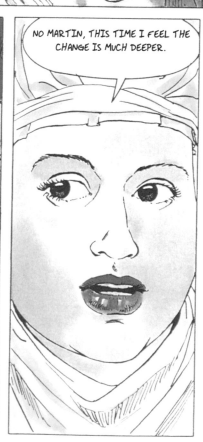

NO MARTIN, THIS TIME I FEEL THE CHANGE IS MUCH DEEPER.

A CHANGE WHICH WAS HELPING IÑIGO SHAPE A PLAN HE WAS NOT YET READY TO REVEAL.

I WILL GO TO JERUSALEM AS A BAREFOOT PILGRIM, EATING ONLY PLANTS FOR FOOD, AND I WILL PERFORM PENANCE IN REPARATION FOR MY PREVIOUS LIFE.

IÑIGO REALISED IT WAS TIME TO SET OFF. PHYSICALLY HE WAS NOT THE MAN HE HAD ONCE BEEN; HIS LIMP WOULD BE WITH HIM FOR LIFE. HIS FIRST GOAL WOULD BE MONTSERRAT, A CENTRE FOR PILGRIMS.

I MUST GO TO NAVARRETE TO SEE THE DUKE OF NÁJERA; HE STILL OWES ME SOME MONEY.

HE WAS TELLING THE TRUTH: THE VISIT TO THE DUKE WOULD BE HIS FIRST STOP. BUT THE EYES OF MAGDALENA, HIS SISTER-IN-LAW, WERE BRIMMING WITH TEARS. SHE SENSED IT WOULD BE MANY YEARS BEFORE THEY WOULD SEE HIM AGAIN

A NEW LIFE IS STARTING FOR ME. THIS TIME NOTHING WILL STOP ME FROM FOLLOWING MY ONE AND ONLY LORD, JESUS CHRIST.

PLEASED TO SEE YOU, SIR. YOU LOOK AS THOUGH YOU'RE OFF TO SEEK YOUR FORTUNE.

WELL SAID, MY GOOD MAN, THE BEST FORTUNE ONE COULD IMAGINE. I AM GOING TO KNEEL BEFORE OUR LADY, THE VIRGIN OF MONTSERRAT.

I DISAGREE WITH YOU ABOUT THAT. I DO UNDERSTAND THAT YOUR LADY COULD HAVE FALLEN PREGNANT WITHOUT A MAN, BUT FOR HER TO CONTINUE BEING A VIRGIN, THAT I JUST CAN'T BELIEVE.

I WON'T TOLERATE SUCH BLASPHEMY!

I MUST FOLLOW THAT UNBELIEVER AND KILL HIM.

ALTHOUGH MY OBLIGATION AS A KNIGHT IS TO KILL WHOEVER OFFENDS MY LADY, A CHRISTIAN MUST NOT SHED ANOTHER'S BLOOD. LET GOD BE MY GUIDE. I WILL RELEASE THE REINS, AND DEPENDING ON WHICH WAY THE MULE HEADS, I WILL EITHER KILL HIM OR LET THE MOOR GO.

PROVIDENCE SAVED THE MOOR AND EASED IÑIGO'S SCRUPLES.

MONTSERRAT WAS THE FIRST STOP ON WHAT WAS TO BECOME A HUGE ADVENTURE.

FOLLOWING THE TRADITION OF THE KNIGHT ERRANT, HE SPENT THE NIGHT IN PRAYER BEFORE THE ALTAR, LEAVING BEHIND THE WEAPONS HE WOULD NEVER USE AGAIN.

HE SWAPPED HIS RICH CLOTHES FOR THE SACKCLOTH OF THE PILGRIM.

HERE, BROTHER, TAKE THESE – YOU NEED THEM MORE THAN I DO.

SIR, WAIT A MINUTE!

WE CAUGHT THIS THIEF WHO STOLE YOUR CLOTHES. IT WAS EASY, HE'S WELL KNOWN AROUND HERE AS A PETTY CRIMINAL. WE GAVE HIM WHAT HE DESERVED.

LET HIM GO, FOR THE LOVE OF GOD. I GAVE THEM TO HIM. THIS POOR MAN IS INNOCENT.

LORD, I'VE FAILED AGAIN. BECAUSE OF MY FOOLISHNESS, I'VE BROUGHT HARM TO THAT POOR MAN; ALL BECAUSE OF MY DESIRE TO BE POOR.

HE CRIED IN HIS TORMENT, FULL OF REMORSE. SOBBING FROM TIME TO TIME, HE SLOWLY MADE HIS WAY TO THE NEXT DECISIVE STOP: MANRESA.

HE THOUGHT HE'D STAY IN MANRESA A FEW DAYS, BUT IN FACT HE STAYED ALMOST A YEAR. AN OUTBREAK OF PLAGUE IN BARCELONA PREVENTED HIM FROM CONTINUING.

IÑIGO BEGGED FOR ALMS WHICH HE DISTRIBUTED TO THE POOR, AND HELPED CARE FOR THE SICK IN THE HOSPICE. HE ATE VERY LITTLE, HARDLY SLEPT, AND CONSTANTLY PRAYED. IN THE TOWN EVERYONE WAS TALKING ABOUT HIM.

HE'S CRAZY.

HE'S A SAINT

LOOK, THE SACKCLOTH MAN!

HIS HEALTH WORSENED. GRAVELY ILL, HE WAS TAKEN IN BY A CHARITABLE FAMILY.

NOW YOU MUST REST AND LO[OK] AFTER YOURSELF. YOU ARE VERY WEAK.

HE IS NOT TO LEAVE HERE.

HE IS A SAINT.

A SAINT...

I WILL NOT LEAVE THIS HOUSE WITHOUT TAKING A RELIC OF HIS.

GOOD HEAVENS! JUST WHO IS THIS MAN?

LITTLE BY LITTLE, WITH THE HELP OF THOSE PEOPLE, IÑIGO RECOVERED HIS HEALTH. MANY PEOPLE CALLED AT THE HOUSE AND HONOURED HIM AS A SAINT.

THE TIME HAS COME FOR ME TO LEAVE FOR JERUSALEM. I WILL NEVER FORGET MANRESA, NOR YOU GOOD PEOPLE.

YOU ARE STILL RECOVERING. STAY A LITTLE WHILE LONGER.

ONCE AGAIN HE WAS ON THE ROAD. AFTER MANY MONTHS OF PRAYER AND PENANCE, HE FOUND TRUE MEANING IN HIS LIFE. HE WROTE DOWN ALL THAT HE EXPERIENCED AND MEDITATED ON, IN A NOTEBOOK WHICH WAS TO BECOME A GUIDE TO HUMAN KNOWLEDGE AND A WAY TO PERFECTION, LEADING TO GOD. HE WOULD CALL IT THE SPIRITUAL EXERCISES.

THANKS TO THE CHARITY OF OTHERS, HE CROSSED THE MEDITERRANEAN ON HIS WAY TO ITALY.

I'M ON MY WAY TO ROME WITH MY SON. IF YOU LIKE, WE CAN TRAVEL TOGETHER.

IÑIGO LOOKED AT THE YOUNG MAN. HE WAS VERY HANDSOME.

WE CAN SPEND THE NIGHT HERE. THE SOLDIERS SEEM FRIENDLY ENOUGH.

IÑIGO BECAME AWARE OF THE EVIL WAY THE SOLDIERS WERE LOOKING AT THE 'YOUNG MAN'.

FROM UNDER THE GUISE OF A BEGGAR, THE BRAVE SOLDIER REAPPEARED.

BACK OFF, YOU SCUM. I WILL NOT ALLOW SUCH AN OUTRAGE.

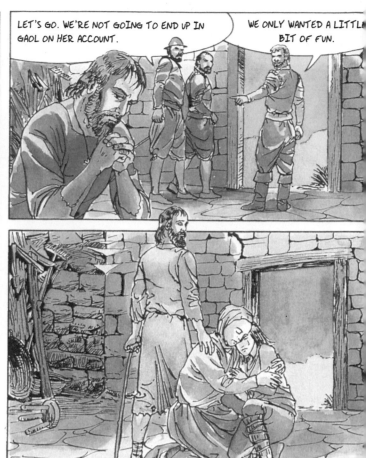

LET'S GO. WE'RE NOT GOING TO END UP IN GAOL ON HER ACCOUNT.

WE ONLY WANTED A LITTLE BIT OF FUN.

THE THREE OF THEM SET OFF TOGETHER IN THE EARLY MORNING. THE WOMEN FELT PROTECTED BY THIS UNKNOWN KNIGHT DRESSED IN BEGGAR'S CLOTHES.

WE ARE CLOSE TO ROME. GO ON WITHOUT ME. I FEEL VERY TIRED.

GOODBYE AND THANK YOU, SIR.

IÑIGO WATCHED THEM WALK ON, AND SIGHED. THE PALE, SHY GIRL REMINDED HIM OF OTHER TIMES WHEN HE HAD BEEN A GALLANT COURTIER. NOW HIS THOUGHTS CENTRED ON ANOTHER GREAT LADY.

HE WAS AT SEA AGAIN, SAILING THIS TIME FROM VENICE TO CYPRUS, AND FROM THERE, TO JERUSALEM. HIS LONG PILGRIMAGE WAS AT AN END.

IÑIGO FINALLY ARRIVED IN THE LAND WHERE CHRIST HAD WALKED.

I HAVE DECIDED TO LIVE AND DIE IN JERUSALEM. I WILL VISIT THE FRANCISCAN HOUSE WITH THESE LETTERS OF RECOMMENDATION.

FILLED WITH EMOTION, HE PRAYED AND CRIED FOR SEVERAL HOURS.

WHEN THE FRANCISCANS FOUND HE WAS MISSING, THEY SENT GUARDS TO SEARCH FOR HIM.

COME ON, CLEAR OFF!

THE RETURN TRIP WAS DANGEROUS AND DIFFICULT. DURING THE VOYAGE A NEW IDEA DAWNED ON HIM.

I WILL STUDY FOR A TIME SO THAT I CAN BETTER CARE FOR SOULS.

MY LORD, THE INQUISITOR, MEXIA, IS HERE FOR HIS AUDIENCE.

MY LORD.

I HAVE SENT FOR YOU SO THAT I MIGHT BE KEPT INFORMED ABOUT CERTAIN EVENTS OCCURRING IN ALCALÁ WHICH WORRY ME GREATLY.

I WANT TO KNOW EVERYTHING IN RELATION TO A CERTAIN IÑIGO DE LOYOLA WHOSE PRESENCE IN THE CITY IS CAUSING SOME SERIOUS UPSET. THEY SAY HE IS OVER 30, AND YET HAS BEGUN STUDYING LATIN IN A SCHOOL FOR BOYS!

BUT WHAT WAS MORE SERIOUS WAS THAT IÑIGO WAS GOING AROUND WITH A GROUP OF YOUNG MEN DRESSED IN CLERICAL CLOTHES, ALTHOUGH THEY WEREN'T YET CLERGY, AND SOME OF THEM WERE BAREFOOT...

AND THEY MET IN HOUSES FOR NIGHTLY DISCUSSIONS, TO WHICH UNACCOMPANIED OR SINGLE WOMEN WERE INVITED, INCLUDING PROSTITUTES.

IÑIGO DE LOYOLA, YOU MUST COME WITH ME. THE HOLY OFFICE REQUIRES YOU FOR AN INTERROGATION.

WE HAVE HEARD THAT AT YOUR MEETINGS SOME WOMEN FREQUENTLY FAINT OR ARE SUBJECT TO SWOONS.

WHEN A WOMAN WHO HAS BEEN A SINNER CHANGES HER LIFE, THE SWOON IS A REFLECTION OF THE SELF-REPROACH SHE FEELS.

IS IT TRUE THAT YOU POINT OUT TO THE WOMEN WHICH SINS THEY SHOULD OR SHOULD NOT CONFESS?

ONLY IN CASES WHERE I FIND THEY ARE SUFFERING FROM SCRUPLES AND NOT REAL SIN... THEN I ADVISE THEM NOT TO MAKE THEIR CONFESSION.

WHY DO YOU ALL WEAR THOSE SAME HABITS IF YOU ARE NOT CLERICS?

OUR HABITS ARE MADE FROM A COARSE WOOLLEN CLOTH AND ARE A SYMBOL OF OUR POVERTY. IF IT BOTHERS YOU THAT THEY ARE ALL THE SAME, WE WILL HAVE THEM DYED IN DIFFERENT COLOURS.

FINDING NOTHING WITH WHICH TO CHARGE HIM, THE INQUISITORS SUSPENDED THEIR HEARINGS. THEY ONLY REMINDED HIM OF THE BAN ON WALKING AROUND BAREFOOT.

GOODBYE, MY BROTHERS AND SISTERS. WE'LL SEE YOU TOMORROW.

WHO ARE YOU? WHY ARE YOU AFRAID TO SHOW YOURSELF?

I'M ASHAMED TO APPROACH YOU. I'M A LOST CAUSE.

NO, NO, QUITE THE OPPOSITE, YOUR HUMILITY AND SINCERITY DO YOU CREDIT. WHAT'S YOUR NAME?

MARIA DE LA FLOR.

MARIA DE LA FLOR CAME MANY TIMES TO IÑIGO FOR ADVICE. HE HAD TO BE PATIENT WITH HER AND CAREFULLY RETRACED HER LIFE STORY SO THAT SHE MIGHT BE REBORN TO A NEW SENSE OF PURPOSE AND VALUE. HE FOUND HER AN OPEN AND EXTREMELY GENEROUS WOMAN. PERHAPS THAT'S WHY SHE HAD BEEN SO FREE WITH HER BODY AND THE VICTIM OF MANY SHALLOW AFFAIRS.

HE WAS THE FIRST MAN WHO DID NOT LOOK UPON HER AS AN OBJECT, WHO SPOKE TO HER OF IDEALS BEYOND MERE PHYSICAL PLEASURE, AND WHO DISCOVERED IN HER AN INNER, VERY SPIRITUAL WORLD.

THE AGENTS OF THE INQUISITION THOUGHT THAT THIS TIME THEY HAD FOUND A REASON TO CHARGE HIM.

33

WE KNOW THAT DURING YOUR MEETINGS YOUR FACES WERE VERY CLOSE, AS IF YOU WERE MARRIED.

WHENEVER I LOOK THAT MAN IN THE EYE, MY SADNESS GOES AWAY.

FREE ONCE MORE, IÑIGO WENT TO SALAMANCA WITH HIS FRIENDS TO PURSUE FURTHER STUDY. THERE HE STRUCK A NEW OBSTACLE IN THE RELIGIOUS DECREES THAT FORBADE ANYONE WHO HAD NOT COMPLETED THEOLOGICAL STUDIES FROM PREACHING THE WORD OF GOD. ON ONE OCCASION, IÑIGO AND HIS COMPANIONS WERE CONFINED TO A MONASTERY BECAUSE THEY WERE CONSIDERED DANGEROUS. IN THE FACE OF SO MANY HARDSHIPS, IÑIGO DECIDED TO SEEK BETTER QUALIFICATIONS AT A MORE RESPECTED UNIVERSITY: THIS TIME HIS DESTINY LED HIM TO PARIS.

AND HERE WERE SOWN THE SEEDS OF WHAT WAS TO BECOME HIS GREAT WORK.

OUR HOUSE IS OPEN TO ALL. MY NAME IS FAVRE, I'M FROM SAVOY AND I'M FINISHING MY PHILOSOPHY STUDIES.

I COULD NOT HAVE WISHED FOR A BETTER COMPANION. I'VE JUST BEGUN MY STUDIES, BUT I HAVE A POOR HEAD FOR BOOKS.

IT'LL BE A PLEASURE TO HELP YOU. MY FRIEND, FRANCIS XAVIER, IS ABOUT TO GRADUATE — YOU'LL BE GOOD FRIENDS SOON, I'M SURE.

I DON'T THINK SO. I PREFER TO FOLLOW MY NEW PROFESSION THAN TO WASTE TIME WITH BEGGARS.

IÑIGO REALISED THAT HE HAD A HARD NUT TO CRACK IN WINNING OVER THIS PROUD YOUNG MAN WHO WAS FULL OF WORLDLY AMBITIONS.

YOU CAN COUNT ON ME. I'LL HELP YOU WITH WHATEVER I CAN.

FRANCIS XAVIER WAS ONE OF THE MOST BRILLIANT YOUNG MEN AT THE UNIVERSITY, NOT JUST IN ACADEMIC PURSUITS BUT ALSO IN SPORT. HIS HOSTILITY TOWARDS IÑIGO CAME IN PART FROM HIS NAVARRAN BACKGROUND: HE COULD NOT FORGET THAT IN THE RECENT PAST, PEOPLE FROM GUIPUZCOA HAD BEEN ALLIES OF THE FACTION THAT HAD FOUGHT AGAINST HIS PEOPLE.

THE DAYS WENT BY IN THAT ROOM WITH THE ICE BETWEEN XAVIER AND IÑIGO STILL UNBROKEN. IÑIGO'S KIND WORDS WERE REBUFFED WITH A CRUEL GUFFAW OR A JIBE FROM THE NAVARRAN.

IÑIGO WAS WORKING LITTLE BY LITTLE ON FRANCIS, AND KEPT TALKING GENTLY TO HIM DESPITE XAVIER'S GRUFFNESS. AN UNEXPECTED LETTER WOULD GIVE EVENTS A DECISIVE PUSH.

HERE'S SOME NEWS FROM HOME.

HOW AWFUL! MY SISTER MAGDALENA HAS DIED.

MY PAIN IS EVEN WORSE, BECAUSE NOW I WILL HAVE TO GIVE UP MY STUDIES.

WHAT'S THAT YOU SAY?

I KNOW THAT WE'VE NOT BEEN CLOSE FOR A LONG TIME, BUT THERE ARE MOMENTS WHEN SUFFERINGS MUST BE SHARED. TELL ME ALL ABOUT IT.

BETWEEN SOBS, XAVIER OUTLINED TO IÑIGO THE REALITY OF THE SITUATION.

IN THE BEGINNING I USED TO ASK FOR A LOT OF MONEY FROM HOME, NOT JUST TO PAY FOR MY STUDIES, BUT ALSO TO MAINTAIN THE LIFESTYLE WHICH MY RANK REQUIRED. WHEN MY MOTHER DIED, MY BROTHERS – DEFEATED OFFICERS DOWN ON THEIR LUCK – DECIDED TO REMOVE MY ALLOWANCE. IT WAS ONLY THE INTERVENTION OF MY SISTER MAGDALENA, AN ABBESS OF THE POOR CLARES, THAT LED THE REST OF THE FAMILY TO KEEP PAYING ME AN ALLOWANCE, ALBEIT RELUCTANTLY

NOW IT'S ALL GOING TO STOP. I'LL HAVE TO DROP MY STUDIES.

ARE YOU CRAZY? I WON'T LET THAT HAPPEN.

YOU ARE NOT ALONE. YOUR PROBLEM NOW BELONGS TO BOTH OF US. FROM HERE ON WE'RE GOING TO TRY AND WORK OUR WAY THROUGH TO A SOLUTION.

IN THIS WAY, THE ICINESS BETWEEN THEM BEGAN TO MELT AWAY, MORE SO WHEN IÑIGO BEGAN TO FIND YOUNG PUPILS FOR XAVIER, WHOSE PAYMENTS SUPPLEMENTED THE MONEY HIS FAMILY COULD NO LONGER PAY.

THESE YOUNG FELLOWS NEED A TUTOR. IT WOULD BE GREAT IF YOU COULD BE THEIR TUTOR.

THIS WAS HOW IÑIGO'S TENACITY OVERCAME XAVIER'S VANITY.

MY SHORT AND INSIGNIFICANT FRIEND, IÑIGO, YOU ARE MUCH GREATER THAN I. I WILL ABANDON EVERYTHING TO FOLLOW YOU.

FOLLOW ME? NO, FOLLOW CHRIST! COME ON, GET UP, YOU GREAT HULK. TODAY IS A HAPPY DAY FOR ME.

THIS INITIAL GROUP OF THREE FRIENDS – IÑIGO, XAVIER AND FAVRE – EXPANDED TO SEVEN, WITH OTHER YOUNG STUDENTS JOINING THEM, ALL INTENT ON FINISHING THEIR STUDIES IN THEOLOGY. THROUGH A VOTE, THEY CONFIRMED THEIR GOAL OF GOING TO JERUSALEM AND DEDICATING THEMSELVES TO APOSTOLIC WORK THERE.

ON THE 15TH AUGUST, THIS GROUP WENT UP MONTMARTRE HILL TO THE CHAPEL CRYPT OF SAINT DENIS AND HIS MARTYR COMPANIONS. DURING MASS THERE, CELEBRATED BY FAVRE – THE ONLY ORDAINED PRIEST AMONGST THEM – THEY WERE ALL UNITED BY A SOLEMN VOW.

A NEW ILLNESS CAME TO CHALLENGE IÑIGO'S ALREADY UNCERTAIN HEALTH: INTENSE STOMACH PAINS, THE CAUSE OF WHICH THE DOCTORS WERE UNABLE TO DIAGNOSE.

THERE'S ONE MEDICINE WE HAVEN'T TRIED YET: A RETURN TO YOUR BIRTHPLACE.

YOU MUST LISTEN TO WHAT WE ADVISE. GO HOME FOR A WHILE.

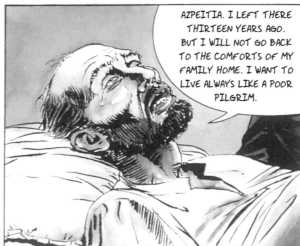

AZPEITIA. I LEFT THERE THIRTEEN YEARS AGO. BUT I WILL NOT GO BACK TO THE COMFORTS OF MY FAMILY HOME. I WANT TO LIVE ALWAYS LIKE A POOR PILGRIM.

ON THE BACK OF A MULE, IÑIGO RETURNED TO GUIPUZCOA. HE KNEW HE WOULD BE WELL KNOWN THERE SO HE TRIED TO REMAIN INCONSPICUOUS. HE REACHED AZPEITIA BY A ROUNDABOUT ROUTE.

ARRIVING AT NIGHT, HE REACHED THE ITURRIOZ INN NEAR AZPEITIA.

I WOULD LIKE A PLACE FOR ME AND MY MULE TO REST.

I'LL SHOW YOU TO YOUR QUARTERS.

I'M JUST DROPPING IN FOR A LITTLE CIDER AND A REST BEFORE HEADING ON TO AZPEITIA.

HI JUAN, YOU'VE COME AT A GOOD TIME.

A MAN'S JUST ARRIVED WHO LOOKS LIKE A BEGGAR, BUT TO ME HE'S GOT THE LOOK OF SOMEONE BORN AND BRED IN AZPEITIA.

LET ME TAKE A LOOK AT HIM.

WELL, WELL, DO YOU KNOW WHO THAT MAN IS? IT'S THE YOUNGEST OF THE LOYOLAS.

OH, I FEEL SO CLOSE NOW TO MY HOME, BUT I MUST BE STRONG AND NOT LET MYSELF BE RULED BY MY FEELINGS.

WHAT'S ALL THAT COMMOTION?

IÑIGO!

MARTIN...

THANKS FOR THE WELCOME, BUT I'M DETERMINED TO GO TO AZPEITIA ALONE. PLEASE LET ME LEAVE.

TO AVOID FURTHER MEETINGS, HE GAVE AZPEITIA A WIDE BERTH BY RETRACING HIS STEPS FOR A SHORT WAY AND STICKING TO WINDING TRACKS. HE FELT A CHILL AS HE RODE OVER FAMILIAR GROUND.

HE SOUGHT SHELTER IN THE HOSPICE AND HELPED THERE IN WHATEVER WAY HE COULD.

IÑIGO'S BEHAVIOUR BRINGS SHAME ON US ALL. WE CANNOT ALLOW A LOYOLA TO GO BEGGING FROM THE PEOPLE.

NONETHELESS, THEY SAY HE'S ACCOMPLISHING GREAT WORK FOR THE POOR AND THE SICK. EVERYONE THINKS OF HIM AS A SAINT.

BUT HE'S HUMILIATING US. HE REFUSES TO LIVE IN THIS HOUSE AND WE'RE TOLD OF HIS ACTIVITIES BY OUR NEIGHBOURS.

WE HAVE NO CHOICE BUT TO GO AND TALK TO HIM.

WHERE IS THAT STUBBORN FOOL?

YOU NEED TO COME HOME. PEOPLE ARE TALKING ABOUT US; IT SEEMS YOU DON'T VALUE OUR HOSPITALITY.

EXACTLY. I WAS THINKING OF LEAVING TOMORROW OR THE NEXT NIGHT.

FINALLY, YOU'VE GOT YOUR COMMON SENSE BACK!

I'M DOING IT BECAUSE OF YOU, MARTIN. I'VE HEARD THAT EVERY NIGHT A WOMAN YOU'RE NOT MARRIED TO SLIPS INTO YOUR ROOM. I'M SO OVERCOME BY THIS SIN OF YOURS THAT I MUST GO AND TALK TO THE WOMAN AND PERSUADE HER NOT TO COME BACK.

THAT'S IT – NOW I'VE HEARD EVERYTHING! AND ME, WHO CAME HERE TO EASE MY CONSCIENCE, I'M THE ONE WHO'S THE LOSER.

IÑIGO SPENT THREE MONTHS IN HIS HOME TOWN, WHERE HE GAINED GREAT RENOWN. HE REALISED, HOWEVER, THE MOMENT HAD COME FOR HIM TO LEAVE, REJOIN HIS COMPANIONS AND PURSUE HIS MISSION.

I DON'T WANT TO BRING YOU ANY MORE BOTHER. I'M LEAVING.

YOU ALWAYS MAKE ME LOOK STUPID. PEOPLE WILL THINK I EVEN DENIED YOU A HORSE FOR YOUR JOURNEY.

OUT OF RESPECT FOR HIS BROTHER, HE AGREED TO RIDE ON HORSEBACK, BUT ONLY AS FAR AS THE BORDER OF GUIPUZCOA, AFTER WHICH HE WOULD CONTINUE ON FOOT.

THIS IS WHERE WE PART COMPANY. PLEASE FORGIVE ME IF I CAUSED YOU TO SUFFER.

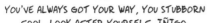

YOU'VE ALWAYS GOT YOUR WAY, YOU STUBBORN FOOL. LOOK AFTER YOURSELF, IÑIGO.

IÑIGO LEFT BEHIND AN AURA OF SANCTITY IN AZPEITIA, A PLACE TO WHICH HE NEVER RETURNED. FOR A LONG TIME MARTIN WATCHED THE FIGURE OF THE SMALL BUT GREAT MAN LIMP OFF INTO THE DISTANCE WITHOUT IÑIGO EVER TURNING AROUND, BECAUSE THEN MAYBE PEOPLE WOULD HAVE SEEN HIS EYES WERE BRIMMING WITH TEARS.

RUMOUR HAS IT THAT THE HORSE IÑIGO RODE WAS ALLOWED TO GRAZE WHEREVER IT LIKED. IT WAS VENERATED AS A RELIC BECAUSE IT HAD ONCE CARRIED A SAINT. THE NOBLE ANIMAL NOW ENJOYED A POSITION OF REAL PRIVILEGE.

ALONE AND ON FOOT, IÑIGO ARRIVED IN VALENCIA, FROM WHERE HE TOOK A SHIP BOUND FOR GENOA. AFTER A HAZARDOUS CROSSING, HE MADE HIS WAY TO BOLOGNA AND THEN ON TO VENICE.

BY LETTER HE REQUESTED THAT HIS COMPANIONS JOIN HIM THERE FROM PARIS. MEANWHILE, HE CONCLUDED HIS THEOLOGY STUDIES AND CONTINUED TO ATTRACT NEW FOLLOWERS.

AT THIS POINT IN THE STORY AN IMPORTANT CHARACTER APPEARED: GIAMPIETRO CARAFA, BISHOP OF CHIETI, CO—FOUNDER OF THE THEATINE ORDER.

I HAVE HEARD OF YOUR ARDOUR AND APOSTOLIC ZEAL, AND WOULD LIKE YOU TO CONSIDER JOINING THE ORDER I HAVE FOUNDED

YOU HONOUR ME, MY LORD.

I'M SURE THAT IN THE ORDER, YOUR DESIRE FOR RENEWAL WILL BEAR FRUIT, BUT YOU MUST FORGET ABOUT THOSE PRACTICES YOU CALL THE SPIRITUAL EXERCISES.

PLEASE EXCUSE MY BOLDNESS, BUT YOUR CONGREGATION SEEMS QUITE CLOSED IN ON ITSELF. THEY LIVE BY BEGGING, BUT DO NOT PRACTISE CHARITABLE WORKS TOWARDS OTHERS.

AND IT DOESN'T SURPRISE ME THAT YOU, AS SUPERIOR OF THE ORDER, DRESS IN FINE CLOTHES AND LIVE IN A PALACE. JUST BECAUSE IT'S ALLOWED, DOESN'T MAKE IT RIGHT. LET ME REMIND YOU THAT SAINT FRANCIS OF ASSISI...

ENOUGH! I WON'T PERMIT A LAYMAN TO TELL A BISHOP WHAT TO DO. I HOPE TO HAVE THE PLEASURE OF MEETING YOU AGAIN SOME TIME.

LATER, CARAFA WOULD BE NAMED A CARDINAL, AND THEN FINALLY POPE, TAKING THE NAME OF PAUL IV.

THE COMPANIONS FROM PARIS ARRIVED IN VENICE WITH EVEN MORE RECRUITS. IÑIGO WOULD BE ALONE NO LONGER. THE GROUP KEPT EXPANDING.

THEIR GOAL WAS JERUSALEM, WHERE THEY INTENDED TO DEDICATE THEMSELVES TO THE CONVERSION OF ALL UNBELIEVERS, READY TO DIE IF NECESSARY FOR THIS CAUSE.

BUT WHEN THEY EVENTUALLY RECEIVED PAPAL PERMISSION TO ENTER THE HOLY LAND, ALL CROSSINGS THERE WERE SUSPENDED BECAUSE OF TENSIONS BETWEEN VENICE AND THE OTTOMAN EMPIRE.

WHAT DO WE DO NOW?

WHILE WE SEEK A SOLUTION, LET'S RETURN TO ITALY. WE WILL TRY TO HELP EVERYONE BY OUR GOOD WORK, AND TEACH CHRISTIAN DOCTRINE, ESPECIALLY TO THE POOR, THE SICK AND THE COMMON PEOPLE.

JUST LIKE JESUS' APOSTLES.

AND IF THEY ASK US WHO WE ARE, WHAT DO WE SAY?

WE'RE NEITHER MONKS NOR FRIARS.

IF WE CALL OURSELVES REFORMED CLERICS, THEY'LL THINK WE'RE LUTHERANS.

WE ARE FRIENDS IN THE LORD. OUR GOAL IS TO LIVE LIKE JESUS AND HIS DISCIPLES. WE ARE COMPANIONS OF JESUS.

THE COMPANY OF JESUS. THIS WAS THE NAME IGNATIUS AND HIS COMPANIONS FIRST GAVE THEMSELVES.

THEIR HOPES OF REACHING THE HOLY LAND DISAPPEARED. XAVIER AND OTHERS CELEBRATED THEIR FIRST MASS. IÑIGO, WHO BY NOW HAD CHANGED HIS NAME TO IGNATIUS, DELAYED HIS MASS, STILL HOPING TO BE ABLE TO CELEBRATE IT IN THE LAND WHERE JESUS HAD WALKED.

YOUR HOLINESS, WE ARE AT YOUR DISPOSAL FOR WHATEVER TASK YOU WOULD LIKE TO ENTRUST TO US. YOUR WISH WILL BE OURS, AS IF WE WERE HEARING THE VERY VOICE OF CHRIST.

I ACCEPT YOUR OFFER. I WANT THE NEW LANDS IN THE EAST TO BE EVANGELISED. I'M ALSO THINKING OF SENDING A MISSION TO ETHIOPIA; AND FURTHERMORE, THERE ARE ALL THOSE SCHISMATICS NOW IN EUROPE WHO MUST BE BROUGHT BACK TO THE TRUE FAITH. I NEED PEOPLE LIKE YOU.

BAD NEWS?

NO, VERY GOOD NEWS. THE POPE HAS GIVEN US NEW MISSIONS BUT I'M WORRIED ABOUT HOW WE WILL ALL REMAIN UNITED, IF WE ARE SO FAR AWAY FROM ONE ANOTHER.

ALTHOUGH RELIGIOUS ORDERS OF THE TIME DID NOT ALWAYS OFFER A FINE EXAMPLE, IGNATIUS AND HIS FRIENDS DECIDED TO ESTABLISH THEIR COMPANY AS A GROUP SHARING A COMMON VISION, BUT FLEXIBLE AND AVAILABLE ENOUGH TO ALLOW THE COMPANIONS TO WORK FREELY IN THE SERVICE OF THE CHURCH. IGNATIUS DRAFTED GUIDELINES WHICH BECAME KNOWN AS THE CONSTITUTIONS, THE WAY OF LIFE OF THE JESUITS.

ONE DAY, THEY CAME ACROSS A SMALL HAMLET CALLED LA STORTA NEAR ROME.

LET'S STOP FOR A LITTLE REST.

HOW ABANDONED IT ALL LOOKS! AND YET WHAT AN ATMOSPHERE OF PEACE I FEEL HERE.

AND HERE HE EXPERIENCED A DIVINE CALLING.

FINALLY, I UNDERSTAND WHAT YOU WANT OF ME. I ASPIRED TO BE A PILGRIM IN JERUSALEM, TO LIVE LIKE YOU AND TO DIE A MARTYR, BUT THAT WAS ALL A DREAM STEMMING FROM MY VANITY. DO YOU WANT ME TO STAY IN ROME? WELL THEN, YOUR SLOW-WITTED IGNATIUS WON'T LET YOU DOWN THIS TIME. I WILL LIVE HERE AND LOOK AFTER MY BROTHERS, AS A SIMPLE PRIEST IN THE COMPANY OF JESUS.

LOOK, FATHER IGNATIUS SEEMS TRANSFORMED.

HE MUST HAVE COME TO SOME IMPORTANT DECISION.

EVERY GROUP NEEDS A LEADER. BEFORE WE ALL LEAVE, WE MUST ELECT OUR HEAD.

IGNATIUS HAS ALL THE VOTES EXCEPT ONE.

THERE MUST BE SOME MISTAKE. LET'S VOTE AGAIN.

DESPITE HIS RELUCTANCE, IGNATIUS HAD TO ACCEPT BECOMING SUPERIOR GENERAL OF THE NEW ORDER. HE HAD WANTED TO SERVE AND NOW HE WAS BEING ASKED TO LEAD. THE TIRELESS WANDERER WOULD NEVER AGAIN LEAVE ROME.

THE YEARS PASSED. HIS FRAGILE HEALTH WAS DETERIORATING.

YOU DON'T HAVE TO IMITATE ME, PEDRO, JUST JESUS.

IS IT TRUE, MASTER IGNATIUS, THAT YOU DON'T LIKE MUSIC?

QUITE THE OPPOSITE, RIBADENEIRA. WHEN I WAS YOUR AGE I LOVED IT, SINGING AND PLAYING LAUDS.

THEN WHY DON'T WE HAVE SOLEMN CHANTS?

BECAUSE IT WOULD MEAN LESS TIME FOR OUR APOSTOLATE.

AND LESS TIME FOR STUDY. WE MUST MEET GOD IN OUR EVERYDAY ACTIVITIES AND NOT JUST IN LENGTHY PRAYERS.

YOU KNOW, I WANTED TO DIE A MARTYR IN JERUSALEM AND NOW HERE I AM: A RESIDENT OF ROME, WHILE OUR COMPANIONS ARE DEVOTING THEIR LIVES FOR CHRIST THROUGHOUT THE WORLD.

THE IMPORTANT THING, PEDRO, IS TO LOVE AND SERVE WHEREVER GOD WANTS US. AND NOW LET'S MAKE OUR WAY HOME, SINCE IT'S NEARLY DINNER TIME AND THE COOK WILL NOT APPRECIATE IT IF I'M NOT THERE TO HELP HIM SET THE TABLE.

ONE MORNING IN THE SUMMER, THEY FOUND IGNATIUS DEAD IN HIS ROOM. HE DIED A DEATH STRIPPED OF ALL CEREMONY. HE DIED ALONE, WITHOUT THE PRESENCE AND TEARS OF HIS COMPANIONS AT HIS BEDSIDE. HIS LEGACY WAS TO SEEK TO FIND GOD IN ALL THINGS AND TO FOLLOW JESUS WHEREVER THE GREATEST NEED COULD BE DISCERNED FOR GOD'S GREATER GLORY. THE DATE WAS 31ST JULY 1556.

I. Iñigo, the youngest child

Iñigo Lopez de Loyola, the future Saint Ignatius, was born in 1491. We are not certain about either the day or the month, but possibly it was around the 1st June, the feast of Saint Iñigo, abbot of Oña (Burgos), for that was the baptismal name he was given.

Iñigo was the son of Beltran Ibañez de Oñaz and Marina Sanchez de Licona, a descendant of the noble Oñaz-Loyola family from Guipuzcoa, or 'the Province', as this area was called until the 20th century. The Loyolas lived in a tower house which was both a residence and a fortress built in stone, like so many others in the Basque country. Its double role as home and castle can be explained by the frequent wars that broke out, firstly between the leading Basque families, then later with the Brotherhood of Towns, towns that were growing at the end of the feudal period.

The Loyolas had been heavily involved in these local wars. Iñigo's grandfather was exiled by the king as a result of one of them and obliged to demolish the upper part of the tower house. When he was pardoned by the sovereign, he was allowed to rebuild the upper floor in brick.

Iñigo was born in this fortress house. Times were calmer, even though old enmities took centuries to disappear, especially in a small isolated valley like the one formed by the Urola River, which linked the neighbouring towns of Azpeitia and Azcoitia. Midway between the two of them, Iñigo was born.

Iñigo was six when his mother died. His father followed when Iñigo was sixteen, and bequeathed all his property and titles to his older son Martin, who became the Lord of Oñaz-Loyola. Martin was not the first-born, but that son, Juan, had been killed in the Milanesado war.

His father, his brother Martin and Martin's wife, Magdalena de Araoz, took care of Ignatius' education. From a young age, being the youngest in the family, he understood that he had to plan for his future, just as his older brothers had

done: Beltran and Ochoa had joined the militia; Hernando had gone to America; and Pedro had become a priest.

Iñigo's childhood was like that of any other boy of noble birth, tempered somewhat, of course, by the fact that he was the youngest and also motherless. His religious education was more pious than profound. The family chapel in the tower house was dominated by a Flemish painting of the Annunciation, a gift from Isabel the Catholic to Magdalena, his brother Martin's wife. It was said to be miraculous.

Iñigo took the tonsure as he approached his teens. In other words, he became a minor cleric. As such he was able to benefit from a certain financial support attached to this church role. But as will be seen in the charge brought against him in Pamplona, his behaviour left a lot to be desired. From the court records it is clear that his way of life, dress and hairstyle were a long way from being those of a churchman.

No one knows what crime was attributed to Iñigo and his brother, Pedro, one day during Carnaval (the time of celebration before Lent). But it was serious enough for them to have to flee and for him to appeal to his clerical status as a way of escaping a conviction.

The impression left by these details of Iñigo's early life is of a somewhat wild, hot-headed young man, who was certainly very aware of the privileges that stemmed from his birth and status as a gentleman.

II. A Young Knight

When Iñigo was 15 or 16, he went to Arevalo to complete his education in the home of Don Juan Velazquez, chief treasurer for the Kingdom of Castile. He was a friend of Iñigo's father and offered to welcome the youngest of the Loyolas as if he were another son. Iñigo must have felt at home there, surrounded by the Velazquez sons, some of whom were around his own age, and living in style.

In the Velazquez' household, he came to know the king and queen and the court. He enjoyed all the privileges of the then high aristocracy. He threw himself into the good life: hunting, jousts, tournaments, soirées, gambling (both cards and dice) and romantic pursuits. Years later, now calling himself Ignatius of Loyola, he would admit to being given over to the vanities of the world at that time and to have committed many youthful indiscretions.

Iñigo had a great liking for music and dancing. He developed a fine, distinctive style of handwriting, and must have read many books of chivalry, the bestsellers of the day. These were ten years of youthful enjoyment, with hardly a thought about the future, as can be seen when disgrace suddenly swept over the Velazquez family, taking both Iñigo and his guardians by surprise. The death of Ferdinand the Catholic was the ruin of the family. The initial decisions of the soon-to-be Charles I contradicted what Don Juan Velazquez thought was best for the proper economic management of the realm, and so Velazquez tried to oppose them by force of arms. Defeated and heavily in debt, he died in 1517.

Iñigo now had no patron. He had nothing. Velazquez's widow gave him some money and letters of recommendation for the Duke of Nájera, Don Antonio Manrique de Lara, an up-and-coming noble. He had supported the future emperor and was viceroy of Navarre. Iñigo became an aide to the duke, whom he accompanied on various royal missions and visits to court. It is possible that this was the time when he glimpsed Princess Catalina of Austria, since biographers believe it was she to whom Iñigo was alluding, when he admitted later that he had met a lady more highly ranked than either a duchess or countess.

In the duke's service, he fought against those who were opposed to Charles I. He thus took part in the siege and conquest of his own city, Nájera, which had rebelled against the king, but not in its later sacking and pillage. The duke also entrusted him with calming other small towns in Guipuzcoa which had also risen. He showed some talent for diplomacy, since his mission proved successful.

Iñigo was not what we would today call a military man or professional soldier. He was a noble gentleman and as such was expected to be skilled with weapons.

Wars in those times were organised differently from those that occur today. When the king of France decided to support the exiled Enrique de Labrit, pretender to the throne of Navarre, the viceroy summoned troops to defend home territory. Among the recruits were Iñigo and his brother Martin, the lord of Loyola. This all happened when Iñigo was thirty. He was still unmarried and his only assets were his personal belongings. With his carefree youth now behind him, he still hoped to win for himself a place of honour in society.

III. The Shattered Leg

Iñigo had an aunt who was a nun, and when she heard of the trouble and adventures her nephew kept getting into, she predicted: "You won't come to your senses, or wise up, until you break a leg!" The good sister could never have imagined that her words would be prophetic. Iñigo was wounded by a cannon ball in the siege of Pamplona, and this would be the beginning of a profound change in his life.

French and Navarran troops, who wanted to restore Enrique de Labrit to the throne, reached the gates of the city without Charles' supporters being able to secure enough men and weaponry to match them. The inhabitants surrendered without a fight, but the Duke of Nájera's men – Iñigo among them – withdrew to the walled citadel.

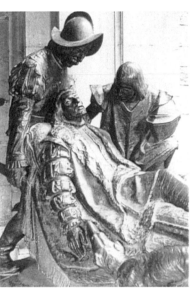

Seeing the imbalance of forces, most of the besieged remnant, including the governor, thought it best to give up without a fight. It would be suicide to try to stand up to a larger army well-equipped with artillery. Iñigo did not agree with this stance. He thought it dishonourable to surrender and tried to convince his companions to fight.

Cannon fire began to batter the fortress on the 20th May, 1521. During the bombardment, a cannon ball struck Iñigo, breaking one leg and leaving the other badly damaged. On the 24th May, with its walls breached and its keenest defender out of action, the castle surrendered.

The enemy chivalrously recognised the bravery of the youngest of the Loyolas and took care of his injuries. But these were so severe, they advised that he be taken back home where he would receive better treatment than in a city at war.

He was carried from Pamplona to Loyola on a stretcher. How hard the journey must have been, with all those fractures and other injuries which, whenever the going got tough, would have triggered unbearable pain.

His reception at home must have been difficult as well. Iñigo was back severely injured, defeated, but with his honour as a knight still intact. His brother Martin couldn't help reminding him that he was a stubborn fool to have stayed in Pamplona when others, like Martin himself, and even the Duke of Nájera, beat a strategic retreat.

His health worsened. Doctors recommended an operation to reset the leg bones which, because of the journey home or the incompetence of the Pamplona surgeons, were out of alignment. Years later, Ignatius called the operation a butchery. However, he showed great self-control during the procedure, holding back his screams while just clenching his fists.

The operation was unsuccessful. Iñigo was on the point of death. He was given the last rites. Everyone thought the end was near. It seemed the bad luck that had plagued his older brothers was to be his lot too. Dead at thirty! A gentleman, certainly, both brave and ambitious. But there was nothing he had done for which he would be remembered. Many must have thought: he deserved it. He just enjoyed himself and had a good time. He won't be any loss really.

IV. The Great Change

Death did not claim him. Iñigo got better, but found his injured leg was shorter, with a pronounced lump below the knee. "Will I limp for the rest of my life? Unthinkable!" How would he be able to ride a horse, accomplish great deeds and pursue the woman of his dreams while a stupid cripple?

At his own request, he underwent a second operation to remove the deformity. The pain was as bad as before. Then he was forced to lie in bed for months while all sorts of weights and devices were used in an attempt to lengthen the leg bone.

Just what does an invalid do when confined to bed? Make all kinds of plans for the future: the deeds he would do for his fair lady, the manner in which he would approach her, the gallant things he would say, and the warrior feats he would dedicate to her.

But Iñigo got bored. His own imagination was not enough. He asked for some books on knights and chivalry for some fresh ideas. There were none in the tower house, just some pious books: a life of Christ and another on the lives of the saints.

Grudgingly, and to pass the time, he began to read them. To his great surprise, he found they were enjoyable. But more than that, when he closed the books, he felt a great sense of peace and joy, the opposite of what he felt when he dipped into the books of chivalry to feed his imagination: they only left him feeling sad and frustrated. This mixture of emotions left him confused.

Furthermore, Iñigo had looked death in the face. He thought back over his past life, the logical thing one does when at death's door with time to reflect. The balance was not positive. From God's perspective, he was a sinner and a bad Christian.

Spurred on by the feelings stemming from his pious reading, he began to wonder: "What if I were to do what Saint Francis and Saint Dominic did?" There was no lack of courage or daring in Iñigo. Of this, we are certain. And so he proposed to himself a very difficult undertaking: to go to Jerusalem barefoot, with plants as his only food, undertaking the same, if not more, penance than the saints had done.

His thinking was clearly competitive: Saint Dominic did this, so I have to do it too. If someone had done it before, then he thought himself equally capable. He dreamed of being the best at this, as he had dreamed of the things in his former life.

The months passed, summer, autumn, winter. Gradually his heart was tending towards God. He decided to make notes from the books he was reading, copying passages from the life of Christ, with the words of Jesus written in red ink and the words of Mary in blue. Copy, then imitate, with the goal of becoming more like the saints. And with that, he was developing a special devotion to the person of Jesus and His Mother.

His brothers Martin and Pedro, and his sister-in-law Magdalena, were worried. No longer did they hear him speak of heroic deeds, romances and glory. Sometimes they found him crying; at other moments totally lost in thought. When they asked questions, he replied evasively.

Early in 1522, Iñigo had recovered enough for him to announce his departure. He said he was headed for Navarrete to visit the Duke of Nájera, and collect what he was owed. The family apprehensively watched him set off: what would become of the youngest of the Loyola family?

V. The Sackcloth Man

On the back of a mule, with his brother Pedro and two servants, Iñigo set out for the Marian shrine of Aranzazu. After giving thanks for his recovery, he farewelled Pedro and headed for Navarrete, as he had told his family. He collected his service pay and paid his outstanding debts. He farewelled his servants and, all alone now, headed for Montserrat.

Iñigo decided to put into practice the idea that had dawned on him at Loyola. Of the three great pilgrimages a Christian could undertake (Santiago de Compostela, Rome and Jerusalem), this last destination seemed to him the most difficult (because of the great distance) and the most dangerous. The Holy Land was in the hands of the Ottoman Empire, which was centred on present-day Turkey, with the political situation so tense that war could break out at any time. In these circumstances, going to Jerusalem was a definite risk.

However, he would not go as a noble, protected by his money and social standing, but instead as an unknown pilgrim. From this moment on, Iñigo began to disguise his identity. He didn't want to receive any favours. He wanted to begin a new life. His past, however, weighed heavily on him.

On the journey through Aragon there was an incident with a Moor, who doubted Mary's virginity. Ignatius' mule, smarter than he was, got him out of trouble by leading him along a different path to the Moor. Before arriving in Montserrat, Iñigo bought coarse, rough sackcloth, a walking staff and a gourd, the pilgrim's standard outfit.

He arrived at the feet of La Moreneta (the Black Madonna of Montserrat) around the 20th March. It took him three days to prepare a general confession of his past life, under the skilled guidance of a monk from the abbey. On the eve of the Annunciation (March 25th), he spent the entire night in the church. It was his vigil of arms as a knight now dedicated to God. He offered up to the Virgin his sword and dagger, gave the mule to the monastery, and his fine clothes to a beggar in the church porch.

In the morning, in disguise, and dressed in the sackcloth of the penitent, he departed by way of Manresa, so as to avoid being recognised by people in the retinue of the future Pope Adrian VI.

A short while later, the Montserrat guards caught up to him. They wanted him to confirm that the beggar, now dressed in his finery, had not stolen the clothes. The incident unsettled Iñigo since his generosity had placed the man in a predicament, and he realised that despite his simple dress, he could not really hide his origin and status.

In Manresa, he sought lodging at an inn for beggars, as just another poor man. He begged for food and lived very austerely. He decided to do away with his image as a gentleman in disguise, by taking little care of his appearance and punishing his body with strict fasting. Soon he looked unkempt and the Manresa children called him 'the sackcloth man'.

But he did not achieve what he had set out to: to move around unnoticed. Soon he earned another nickname: 'the holy man'. And there were extraordinary rumours spreading about his identity, the riches he had left behind, and the sins that had driven him to such penance.

Nor did Manresa remain a place of 'peace'. His spirit began to be assailed by all sorts of contradictory feelings. He devoted much time to prayer and sacred reading. He subjected himself to strong penance. And still he found no peace. He doubted God's mercy and his own endurance: 'Will I have to put up with this for the rest of my life? Has God forgiven me?' One day, so great were his anxiety and confusion that he was on the point of committing suicide, by throwing himself through a window.

It had seemed to him that being a saint depended solely on one's will and strength. Iñigo discovered that God was not to be served or satisfied by whatever a person planned or decided of his own account,

VI. What God Wills

That first spell in Manresa was his low point. At Loyola he had developed the habit of committing to paper whatever came into his mind. And so he began to realise, reading over his notes, that the range of his state of mind and spirit held a meaning. That God was showing him His will in this way. His holding back from a deep and sincere conversion appeared at times to be masked by good intentions. At other times, his fasting and excessive penance, far from helping him pray, actually blocked him from praying effectively.

Without knowing it, Iñigo was making the Spiritual Exercises. Through prayer and contemplation of the Gospels, the person of Christ was captivating him, and he was adopting Christ's attitudes and endeavouring to make his entire life conform to Christ's life. The experiences of those days, carefully recorded, formed the basis of his Spiritual Exercises, one of the most influential books in the history of the church. He would revise a few aspects, add and delete things, but the Ignatian method for discerning the will of God and holding close to the person of Jesus was already present in his notes.

At Manresa, Iñigo realised God was treating him as a teacher does a pupil: God was teaching him how to serve. One day, while walking along the banks of the Cardoner River, he experienced great enlightenment.

Everything seemed new and refreshingly clear, as if he were seeing things for the first time.

Copy and imitate. At Loyola, this was what he had thought the Christian life was about. Be like the saints, imitate Jesus. Now he discovered that everyone has a particular vocation. And that God will reveal it in many different ways. Christians are to recognise and follow the mission that God has entrusted to them.

Where was this all leading him? Iñigo was still thinking of going to Jerusalem. Not to achieve great feats, but simply because it was the land where Jesus had walked. If he lived as a poor person, free of material concerns, it wouldn't be for the sake of doing penance, but because that was the way Christ had lived. And so he began to reach out to others, caring for the sick and the needy, and seeing to their spiritual needs, because Jesus had cured the sick, preached, and freed people from their sins.

In this way the pilgrim committed himself to God, ready at any time to follow His inspiration. He did not know where it would lead him. But until he knew otherwise, he would continue his course to Jerusalem. He even dreamt of dying there, like Jesus, while proclaiming the Good News to all.

He spent nearly a year in Manresa. He was welcomed into several homes and spent some time in the Dominican convent. He also withdrew to a cave where he prayed and did penance. (Over this place today, a Jesuit church stands). More importantly, he began to talk to those willing to listen to him about spiritual matters.

From Barcelona he embarked for Italy. He managed to get free passage, though the ship's master demanded that he bring his own food. This caused Iñigo some uncertainty, since he preferred to place himself totally in God's hands. His confessor suggested a solution: he would bring his own food, but it would be whatever he had gained from begging.

In March 1523, a year after he had left the tower house, alone and poor, Iñigo was off on his voyage. No one recognised in the humble, wasted pilgrim the once elegant and handsome youngest child of the Loyola family.

VII.   The Pilgrim

They arrived in Italy in five days with a good following wind. To travel to the Holy Land, travellers needed papal permission. And so Iñigo decided to walk to Rome. On the way, he met a mother who had dressed her daughter as a young man to avoid unwelcome attention from other travellers. The ruse was of little help. One night at an inn, a group of soldiers tried to rape the women. Iñigo spared them any real harm by calling on his former soldierly skill.

In Rome, he had no trouble obtaining a papal visa. He took it with him to Venice from where ships left for the Holy Land. Italy was affected by the plague, and Iñigo's unattractive appearance did not make things easier for him. He suffered from hunger and other torments.

Once in Venice, thanks to a Spanish noble, the Doge granted him free passage for July of that year. Meanwhile, Iñigo lived in the open by begging, his one refuge being his trust in God.

The voyage to Palestine was long and difficult, as the ship was often becalmed. The crew engaged in open, sexual activity and Iñigo abhorred their conduct. The sailors did not take too kindly to his reproaches and at one stage threatened to abandon him on an island.

Finally, on the 24th August 1523, they docked at Jaffa. The pilgrims kissed the ground, sang the *Te Deum* and *Salve Regina*, and continued on their way, accompanied by Franciscan friars and escorted by Ottoman soldiers.

Direct contact with the land where Jesus had walked stirred strong emotions in Iñigo. With his eyes wide open, he took in every detail of the places he had read about in scripture. Years later, when he set down his contemplations on the life of Christ, he recalled the most precise details of the places he had visited.

Because of the political situation, pilgrims could only visit Jerusalem and its environs (including Bethlehem, Jericho and the River Jordan). Iñigo intended to stay there. He had with him letters of recommendation to the Father Superior of the Franciscans who looked after the Holy Places. These were of no use to him, nor did his powers of persuasion help. The friar threatened him with excommunication if he persisted in his enterprise.

There was no alternative but to accept his expulsion from the country. However, on the eve of his departure from Jerusalem, he managed to sneak out one last time, alone and without telling anyone, to the Mount of Olives. They sent people out looking for him. The servant who found him was annoyed and tied him up. Iñigo recalled that in this very place, they had also arrested Jesus, and he experienced intense emotion.

A mere twenty days in the Holy Land! He who had dreamed of spending the rest of his life there! During the long, hazardous voyage back to Italy, he had time to ask himself: 'What am I going to do now? What does God want me to do, if He didn't want me to remain in Jerusalem?'

Hoping perhaps for better times, and eventually a removal of the ban on living in the Holy Land, he returned to Venice. It was already January 1523, and a deep cold snap had descended on the region. In the city of canals, the news ended up chilling his spirit: there would be no possibility of returning to Jerusalem for a long time.

VIII.   A Controversial student

Iñigo noticed that he brought much consolation to people with whom he came into contact. And thinking of how he might best use his time after returning from the Holy Land, he decided to devote himself to study. This was what people advised him to do after they felt better talking with him. The Church was full of self-styled gurus and false preachers, so without any theological training, Iñigo might have been mistaken for one of them.

Iñigo set off again. He left Venice for Barcelona, where he arrived in February 1524. There at the age of thirty-three, Iñigo began studying Grammar and Latin. At first he took private lessons, then later he attended a class with other teenage students who made him the object of their jokes and jibes. Iñigo pressed on. He continued to beg for alms and talked of spiritual matters to whoever was willing to listen.

He spent two years at his preparatory studies. His teachers advised him to enrol at the University of Alcalá de Henares to study Arts. At the age of 35, he arrived there. On foot as ever, without any money, a beggar trusting solely in God.

His fifteen-month stay in Alcalá was very hectic. He gained little from his studies as he was caught up in three hearings before the court. What happened? It seems that Iñigo spent more time in his apostolic work than at his studies. Very soon he attracted a circle of admirers, most of them women, who followed the spiritual advice he gave them.

The first conflict stemmed from his dress. Three young followers of Iñigo had come from Barcelona wearing the same sackcloth as he. The inquisitors were not pleased since this resembled a religious habit, and the young men were clearly not ordained religious. Iñigo and his followers, who declared they wanted to live like the apostles, were directed to change their attire. They obeyed this decree of the ecclesial court.

The second enquiry resulted from women in the upper class coming to him for spiritual direction, but doing so secretly. This secrecy aroused suspicion. The investigation remained private and so no formal charge was recorded.

The third case was more serious. Iñigo was imprisoned. There was no strict isolation, for he was still allowed contact with people close to him. But he was jailed for 42 days. The inquisitors questioned him about what today we know as the Spiritual Exercises, which Iñigo had begun to use with his visitors so as to help them live a better Christian life.

The sentence was severe and he was required to wear normal clothing and not to engage in spiritual direction with anyone, either privately or publicly. The reason was that the *Iniguistas*, as he and his followers were called in Alcalá, did not have enough training and could therefore lead people into error.

The clothing requirement mattered little to Iñigo. What did worry him was the directive to stop his flourishing apostolate. And so he went to speak to the Archbishop of Toledo in person. The Archbishop was a wise man and advised him not to return to Alcalá, but to continue his studies in Salamanca.

At the famous university he again got into difficulties right from the start. Within a few days he was imprisoned again and brought to trial. It was the same sentence as at Alcalá: he kept his freedom, but he could not preach. Iñigo soon made his mind up. He decided on a change of scenery and would complete his studies in Paris. His companions promised to follow him, but none did.

Iñigo had found that his spiritual experiences were helpful to others. And he had no wish to stop just because of some misunderstanding.

IX. Friends in the Lord

Iñigo spent seven decisive years in Paris. He arrived alone in February 1528, and would not leave alone again until April 1535. But by this time he was a Doctor of Philosophy and had completed high-level studies in theology. He had a group of followers who were committed to his way of living and overall vision.

In Paris, he continued to live by begging, but he realised that he could not beg from day to day as this would undermine his studies. Thanks to donations from female benefactors and money he raised during holiday visits to the Netherlands and England, he was able to fund his stay at the Sorbonne.

Years later, when drafting the Jesuit Rule, he agreed that novices could live on a fixed amount during their period of studies, with a less strict interpretation of their vow of poverty. This was an insight drawn from his experience.

Soon after he arrived, he caused a bit of a stir. Three Spanish students completed the Exercises with Iñigo. When they finished, they gave away all their belongings to the poor and came to live with him in the pilgrims' hostel. This caused quite a commotion at the university, as all three were well known. He was accused of being a seducer of young men. Peer pressure led them to give up living by gospel values.

S. IGNATIVS
PARISIIS IN MONTE MARTYRVM
FESTO ASSVMPTIONIS B.V.MARIÆ
CVM IX SOCIIS PER PRIMA VOTA

But Iñigo was not discouraged. He kept winning over students, beginning with his roommates in the college where they lived. They were the Savoyard, Favre, and the Navarran, Francis Xavier. The latter took a lot of winning over, but once a follower, he became one of his most fervent companions. Gradually, a group was forming: Lainez from Soria, Salmeron from Toledo, Bobadilla from Palencia, and the Portuguese Rodrigues.

All completed the Exercises with Iñigo and all had the same desire: to help other people and go to the Holy Land and evangelise amongst the people there. They were friends in the Lord and wanted to be close to Jesus, even physically, hence their determination to be in Jerusalem. Their ideal was to preach out of their poverty and live in the manner of the apostles.

Another feature that distinguished them was their generosity. They offered themselves in such a way as to be of most service to God and their neighbour, for the most difficult of assignments. This was the sense of the phrase that Iñigo often repeated: 'For God's greater glory'. One could not be a timid follower, only a passionate one, open to all possibilities.

And so the seven companions decided to seal their commitment. They gathered in the church at Montmartre on the 15th August 1534. Favre celebrated mass, the only one at the time who was a priest, and they all made vows of poverty, chastity and of going on pilgrimage to Jerusalem. If they could not achieve this, they would place themselves at the Pope's disposal. This was the birth of the future Company of Jesus.

In a Paris caught up in the currents of the Protestant reform, this small group of men seemed uncontroversial. They were intent on living as good Christians, in other words following Jesus' poverty, simplicity and freedom. Without realising it, they had begun the true reform of the Church.

Iñigo changed his name to Ignatius. We don't know why. Maybe he Latinised his name on graduating from the University. His health was not good. He was paying for his excessive penances and his very frugal lifestyle. His companions, along with his doctor, advised him to return to his home town and rest. They agreed to meet again in Venice in two years' time to attempt the crossing to Jerusalem.

Ignatius was on the road again, though this time on horseback. The companions had insisted. He returned to Loyola. It had been thirteen years since he had left the tower house. He had no intention of being recognised by the locals.

X. Preaching in Poverty

The Ignatius who arrived in Azpeitia in 1535 was very different from the one his fellow country people remembered. His brother Martin had arranged for him to be accommodated in his home and sent a party out to welcome him. Ignatius changed his route to avoid it and entered the town secretly. He headed straight to the hospice for the destitute.

Martin was not impressed at his brother's actions. It was not fitting that a Loyola should share lodgings with beggars. But Ignatius would not relent. From his first moments, he devoted himself to teaching the catechism to the children and sorting out some notorious local moral abuses. Among those was the fact that his brother had a mistress.

While others clamoured for reform and cleansing in the Church, Ignatius chose a direct and simple method: the personal conversion of each person. This was how he proceeded with the companions he had gathered round him. And that was how he was acting now. He attacked at the point where the Church of his day was the most vulnerable: its overwhelming eagerness for riches and power, its ecclesiastical pomp, the corrupt life of the clergy, and the neglect and carelessness with which it prepared people for the religious life.

He did not try to denounce heretics or burn them at the stake, he simply invited people to move beyond their mistakes in a spirit of love. He wanted to reform the lives of Christians who were not living up to the name. He was not interested in the theories of Erasmus or Luther; he stuck to simple Gospel values.

Ignatius preached and taught catechism to children and illiterate people. He asked for nothing in return. He lived as a poor man, from alms. He looked after the marginalised of his time: beggars, the sick, plague victims, prostitutes and orphans. And he respected their freedom. It was said of him that he knew how to move people to want to change their ways. Throughout his life, he managed to defuse numerous conflicts. In his home town too he exercised his gift for reconciling the bitterest enemies.

This brief stay of some three months in his home town foreshadowed the way he worked apostolically in Rome. He never changed his manner of proceeding: he looked after Jews who were being persecuted, young people at risk, children, sick people, famine victims when famine struck the Eternal City, and preaching in the streets, and tapping into his talent for resolving conflicts and disagreements.

From Azpeitia, he went by way of several places in Spain, visiting the families of his Paris companions and sorting out certain matters. In October 1535, he set sail for Genoa, then travelled on to Venice where he arrived by the end of the year. While awaiting the arrival of his companions from Paris, set for 1537, he rounded off his theology studies and, as always, did good work with those he met.

He became aware of a variety of religious movements, from almost heretical groups to a new order called the Theatines, of which Bishop Carafa was a co-founder. The bishop tried to win Ignatius over to the order, but Ignatius disagreed with Carafa's lifestyle and did not like the enclosure its members were bound to.

With all this, he took various people through the Exercises. Someone from Malaga, Diego de Hoces, joined him, and so when the companions arrived in Venice from Paris in January 1537, the group had increased considerably. Besides Hoces, there were also Jay, Codure and Broet who had linked up with the first six in the town of Sena. And there were still more around Ignatius who were keen to join the group.

All together at last, it was time again to attempt the perilous crossing to Jerusalem, which they had all taken a vow to do.

XI. Companions of Jesus

They needed the Pope's permission to set out on pilgrimage for the Holy Land. Before requesting it, Ignatius wanted to put his Paris graduates to the test, sending them into the hospitals and shelters where they had to tend the sick and the destitute: moving from sublime theology to the harsh reality of caring for lepers, plague victims, syphilitics and the dying.

After their two-month stay in the hospitals, Ignatius sent them to Rome for a papal blessing. They would be travelling on foot for four months, in extreme poverty. Ignatius wanted companions who were used to renouncing themselves, dependent only on the hands of God.

Contrary to what they feared, they found all doors in Rome open to them. They obtained the desired permit, and furthermore, the authorisation to be ordained priests. Happily they returned to Venice with the news. But Ignatius greeted them with the sobering news that no ship would leave for the Holy Land that year with pilgrims.

They raised their spirits by taking public vows of poverty and chastity, and went around in twos and threes preaching Christian doctrine and praying.

In the autumn of 1537, they were all ordained, except for Ignatius, perhaps because he was still confident he would celebrate his first mass in the land of Jesus.

As Venice was at war with the Ottoman Empire, and the chances of a quick end to the conflict were remote, they wondered what they would do in the meantime. They decided to place themselves at the Pope's disposal, as they had promised at Montmartre. Ignatius, Favre and Lainez would go to Rome to offer their services to the Vicar of Christ. Meanwhile, the others would be scattered throughout the towns of Italy, much like the 72 disciples in the Gospel.

Before they split up, they agreed on the name they would call themselves if they were ever asked: 'companions of Jesus'. This seemed the most appropriate name, given their situation and spirit. Their goal would be to follow in the footsteps of the apostles and disciples, living together with a sense of detachment, fraternity and freedom. It was another way of expressing the tag 'friends in the Lord' they had coined in Paris.

About 15 kilometres from Rome, Ignatius underwent a profound spiritual experience. He left the road and separated from Favre and Lainez to pray in the rundown chapel of La Storta. He felt that God was telling him: 'I will be favourable to you in Rome'. Ignatius understood the significance of these words: God did not want to be served in Jerusalem, but in Rome. And immediately he dropped the idea of remaining in the Holy Land, his dream since the long-ago days of his convalescence in Loyola.

Once again Ignatius lived by what he had learned at Manresa: that God has a concrete mission for each person and that he or she will be shown it in every aspect of their life. God speaks to us in many ways. It is up to each person to recognise and accept God's will. Sometimes God's voice comes in a striking way such as at La Storta. But in the majority of cases, God comes to us via happenings and events that we must discern, with the help of the Church and the Christian community.

Ignatius would use one of these privileged ways to find out the will of God: the Pope. He would prostrate himself at his feet and ask: "What do you want the Companions of Jesus to do?"

XII. The Branches and the Trunk

The first thing Ignatius and his companions did in Rome was to put themselves at Pope Paul III's disposal. He must have been surprised to hear that they would work for no reward, when so many others were badgering him for honours and privileges. He assigned them pastoral duties in Rome.

The winter of 1538-39 was extraordinarily cold, and hunger afflicted the city. The companions of Jesus worked tirelessly to meet the needs of the poor. Their open and generous involvement earned the sympathy of all. It was during that Christmas that Ignatius celebrated his first mass.

The Pope asked Broet and Rodriguez to go to Siena. The missions the Pope entrusted to them raised a question: to remain united, would they have to become a religious order, or would they be freer if there were no formal links between them?

They all devoted many months of prayer and reflection to finding an answer. Finally, they agreed to become a religious order, called the Company of Jesus. They also agreed that they would not have to wear

a distinctive habit, nor engage in liturgical prayer in common or pre-established penances. The Pope gave his verbal approval to the venture and a year later, on the 27th September 1540, put it formally in writing. They had to elect a superior and draft a rule.

The vote was cast in favour of Ignatius, who resisted accepting it. Finally, he had no alternative but to accept the unanimous vote of his companions. Then he turned his attention to writing the Constitutions of the Order and to directing its first steps. The growth of the group had become quite spectacular, and the Pope kept assigning them to more and more complicated missions.

Ignatius had wanted to accept some of these himself, but the others would not let him leave, so he gradually saw his first companions set out for different destinations and countries: Favre to Germany, Bobadilla to Naples, Rodriguez to Portugal, Xavier to India, Lainez and Salmeron to the Council of Trent...

Branches were extending throughout the known and unknown world: even Ethiopia requested a group. The Company opened houses in Germany, France, Spain, Portugal and Japan. The former wanderer, Ignatius, was now based in Rome: directing, advising, encouraging and writing. He wrote many letters and instructions to those who were leaving for overseas service, or who were already working far from home. And he completed his drafting of the Constitutions. Despite all this, he still sought to answer the needs of the poor, the sick and the persecuted. He also resolved conflicts and and reconciled enemies.

The Company of Jesus became a group of priests who were freely available to respond to the needs of God's people and the Church, whatever the place or time: they had to be ready for whatever task the Vicar of Christ entrusted to them. They were bound to the Pope by a special vow of obedience. From Ignatius' time on, they devoted themselves to education, to evangelisation in distant lands, to intellectual pursuits, to pastoral involvement and to care of the marginalised.

All Jesuits (as members of Ignatius' order were eventually called) make the Spiritual Exercises over a month, and in so doing become better prepared to work as modern day apostles of Jesus, meeting and serving God in all sorts of ways, "to the greater glory of God", as Ignatius urged.

In the last years of his life, Ignatius suffered from a variety of illnesses which affected his liver, kidney, lungs and arteries. As a result, he died early on the morning of the 31st July 1556. By then, the Company of Jesus already had more than a thousand members. For 500 years, in spite of hardships that led to its temporary suppression, the Company has served the Lord Jesus Christ and the Church. Today's Jesuits continue to serve the Church in the same spirit of that nobleman who was born Iñigo de Loyola and ended up being called Saint Ignatius of Loyola.

Take, Lord, receive all my liberty,
my memory, my understanding and my entire will.
All that I am and all that I possess
You have given me:
I give it all back to You
to be used according to Your will.
Give me only Your love and Your grace;
These are enough for me,
and I will desire nothing more.

JESUIT – SAINT IGNATIUS LOYOLA – 16TH CENTURY

Timeline

1491   Probable year of Ignatius' birth at Azpeitia in Spain's Basque country. His original name was Iñigo Lopez de Loyola.

1506   Entered court service as a page in Arévalo, Spain.

1507   Iñigo's father died.

1517   Iñigo became an assistant at the court of Antonio Manrique, Viceroy of Navarre.

1521   Iñigo wounded during the defence of the fortress-city Pamplona against the French. Taken back to Loyola close to death, he found great comfort reading about the life of Christ and the lives of the saints.

1522   Iñigo became a pilgrim, giving away his earlier life as a soldier and courtier. He went to the famous shrine to Mary at Montserrat, then on to Manresa, where he recorded his experiences in a notebook, which came to be known as the 'Spiritual Exercises'.

1523   Sailed from Barcelona to Rome, walked to Venice and embarked for the Holy Land. Church authorities did not allow him to stay, so he headed back to Barcelona.

1524   With no clear plan in mind, he began studies at Barcelona.

1526   Studied at Alcalá, Spain. Iñigo and his companions led others through the Spiritual Exercises. They came under suspicion from church authorities.

1528   Continued university studies in Paris. Iñigo was befriended by roommates Pierre Favre and Francis Xavier.

1534 – 15 August: Ignatius (as Iñigo was now called), Favre, Xavier and four other companions pronounced religious vows at a church in Montmartre. They agreed to place themselves before the Pope, ready to go anywhere they were needed.

1537   Ignatius ordained priest at Venice in Italy. Companions' dream of travelling to Jerusalem ended by war. They journeyed to Rome. Ignatius had vision at La Storta (near Rome).

1538   Ignatius and Companions offered themselves to Pope Paul III. Ignatius' First Mass on Christmas Day.

1539   Discussion about Companions becoming a new religious order. Their foundational rules or Institute approved by Pope on 3 September.

1540   Pope Paul III approved the Society of Jesus (Jesuits) as a new order in the Church.

1541   Ignatius elected first Superior General.

1548   Paul III approved use of the Spiritual Exercises.

1550   First text of the Constitutions—guidelines for their way of proceeding—is presented. Ignatius continued to refine them through prayer and reflection.

1556   Ignatius died on July 31 in Rome.

Further reading

Coleman, G   *Walking with Inigo – A Commentary on the Autobiography of St Ignatius* (Anand: Gujarat Sahitya Prakash, 2001).

Grogan, B *Alone and on Foot: Ignatius of Loyola* (Dublin: Veritas, 2009).

O'Malley, JW *The First Jesuits* (Cambridge: Havard University Press, 1995).

Saint Ignatius of Loyola: Personal Writings, translator and notes by J Munitiz and P Endean (London: Penguin, 2004).

Tylenda, JN   *A Pilgrim's Journey: the Autobiography of Ignatius of Loyola* (San Fransisco: Ignatius Press, 2001).